transplant

transplant

POEMS

SHIRLEY RICKETT

FLOWERSONG BOOKS
AN IMPRINT OF
VAO PUBLISHING

DONNA, TX

ISBN 10: 0692354336
ISBN 13: 978-0692354339

FlowerSong Books
An imprint of VAO Publishing
A division of Valley Artistic Outreach
4717 N FM 493
Donna, TX 78537
www.flowersongbooks.com

First printed edition: April 2015

contents

i   Dedication

ii Acknowledgments

1   Finding the New Year

2   At a Lake in the Burbs

3   Our Canada Geese

5   Night Train

7   Aging

8   Still Moving

10 RV

12 Minorities

13 Happy Palms

14 Two Transplants

16 New Eden

17 Car-Watcher in a Power Wheelchair on a Busy Street

18 Borders

20 The Birds at Happy Palms

21 Post-Christmas in the Valley

22 I Don't Know My Home

23 The People at Table 12

25 Good Friday

26 A Cool Easter

27 How to Move in the World

28 The Real Auntie Em Lives at Pleasant Grove

29 Self-Talk

30 Peeling a Papaya

31 Official Buildings

32 Rancho Lomitas

35 Somewhere in South Texas

36 Breaking News

37 Taking Pictures of People Taking Pictures of Fields of Sunflowers

38 Not Your Kentucky Bluegrass in South Texas

39 We Came from Underground

40 Interval

41 "Eyes Wide Open"

42 Evening News

43 The Exile

44 "Waiting"

45 The Camps
46 Mead, Kansas, July
47 Peace
48 Things
49 Dressed in New Clothes, Truth Goes Incognito
50 Shadow
51 Red
52 Late Afternoon
53 By Guadalupe River
54 Sugar Cane
55 First Dove of Summer
56 An Island Where a World Began
57 After Hurricane Ike
58 Allotment
59 In the Dermatologist's Office
60 After You Left
61 María Luisa
62 Poetry Reading
64 Creative Writing Class
65 Great Blue Heron
66 Quinta Mazatlán
67 Etude
68 In Living Every Day
69 What Holds
70 My Husband Washing Dishes
71 On the Back Porch
72 The Bell Inside
74 Awake at 3 am
76 Possum in a Cage
77 A Wall of Windows
78 Yard
79 Where We Live Now
80 Road Trip
81 Last Leg—Driving Texas to the Valley
82 Breath of Words
84 How the World Grows Old
85 The Best Part of the New Year

87 Author Biography
89 Catalog

For Toby, Mark, Melinda, Paul, and Amy

acknowledgements

My thanks and appreciation to the editors of the following journals, magazines, and anthologies:

- *La Noria*, "Last Leg—Driving Texas to the Valley," "New Eden," "Where We Live Now," "Minorities," "Road Trip," "Red," "Good Friday," "Cool Easter."
- *Imagination and Place: Seasonings*: "Rancho Lomitas," "Yard."
- *Boundless: The Anthology of the Rio Grande Valley International Poetry Festival*: "Taking Pictures of People Taking Pictures of Fields of Sunflowers," a Pushcart nomination, "Sugar Cane."
- *Poetry at Round Top*: "Evening News," "The Bell Inside."
- *The Sixth Surface: Steven Holl Lights the Nelson-Atkins Museum*, "Waiting."
- *Valley Town Crier* and *Texas Civil Rights Review:* "The Camps."
- *Interstice*: "Peeling a Papaya."
- *New Borders*: "By Guadalupe River."
- *The Kansas City Star*: "Great Blue Heron."

Lines from "We Really Are Not Mestizos Any More" by Enesto Dueñas used in "Poetry Reading" with permission.

My gratitude to the First Tuesday Poets who meet at The Writers Place in Kansas City, Missouri, and to poets Katie Hoerth, Diana Dominquez, Deborah Kroman, and readers, Ashley Hodgson and Maryfrances Wagner.

finding the new year

It didn't appear
on the patio where we sat with the last
couple to leave, nor in the sky still
popping with chrysanthemums and noise.

It wasn't conversation
that seemed to ignore the vast turning
of another part of the still new decade
in a still new century, talk that went on—

—a trickling faucet,
just like any other day speaking of the plain
sense of things, passing time, telling stories.
The chairs and table had not changed.

We were the same
except for displacement in Heraclitus'
river, entering   it once more, avoiding stones,
our very lives imperceptible to each other.

It came with empty
glasses loaded on a tray and I saw their faces,
how lovely and human, and the smudged glasses,
the flowers of used napkins, called my name.

at a lake in the burbs

Lawns preen
like well-tended peacocks,
or women who can't let hair go,
or a tan, or what their lives seem.

Voluptuous hostas spill
over on grass, tell secrets
of tree and wind. A single
robin seems drunk with spring.

Over here a driveway cures
strung with yellow tape
that stutters *caution caution*
and here, a vacant lot covered

with milkweed, clumps of purple
bursting into clover, while low,
new weeds stay sober. Backyards

run like children
down to docks and water.
Geese cruise, deserted boats dawdle.
Overcome with riches, paradise can mend

itself. Shade trees hold secret meetings—
(can't tell the weeds from acceptable plants).
Low cool events are sensed not seen:
dark leaves something rubs against.

our canada goose

Men addled eggs this spring—
still the young of three families

trip behind parents in the grass, sail
so close to mothers they are hardly visible

on water. One couple waited
for eggs that never hatched.

They haunt the webbed tracks
of families with goslings, confused.

Their white chin straps
tighten each time they strain

their necks, search the taller grass
just to make sure.

night train

All the names of God I know
churn inside the train's long wail.
There is no sound like it.

My uncle rode the top
of a car on the day
he turned sixteen.

My mother would shiver
at that sound. Who remembers
her long blue dress,

her poverty? In Appalachia
my father heard the night train,
echoes he left that flapped

like a shirt on a clothesline.
Whippoorwills and trains
share the darkness, a shape

I now know has always been there.
I watch the names go
to the next would-be sleeper:

Yahweh, Elohim, Gaia …
A nightjar stays to remind us
how wide is the night sky.

no family bible

I

In the mix potatoes and bare feet,
whips and spurs, blood and peat, sweat
and work, crying babies, big-boned
women, Swedes leaning back to the sky,

a knife to skin buffalo, German precision,
boiled food, muslin and linen, hands made
to grip things, twist out a life, sorrow,
poverty and will, always the will.

When we don't know, when there's no
website for lost names, we make lives
for these immigrants from words heard
and not written down, from the crystal

in an eye, from the frown on a face,
a far-away look, and the songs they
all know but not the origin.
They were just always there.

II

Two sheets like parchment with names
arranged like a pine tree, a bare angle
suggests marriages, children, but clear
enough for memory to pass like the moon

emerged from a beach of dark clouds.
Floating alone is Catherine Lair.
Birth and death dates ride together
as she must have in a fine carriage.

Deep in the Georgia soil that grew the corn,
in molecules that once were a barn, in dust
long gone to the sea speaks the record
of Louis G. Smith's conception.

Family legend holds Catherine and a Cherokee
man tighter than the bonds of paper
stronger than words or records, seals
them as parents with progeny.

III

And what of my great-grandfather,
my native American ancestor?
We see him at dinner with extended family,
startled at the first taste of betrayal,

the pounding at the door, the family poked
with bayonets, forced to leave all behind
like Jews or Japanese Americans,
a trail northwest to a stockade

and death everywhere on the way.
Family threads weave among the larger
family into a blanket of names and bones,
stardust spread before the old moon.

aging

What clock ticks in which firmament?
       Which star describes the end
              of a life or the birth of new one

from our puny point of view? Do you remember
       your first orange? Will you love
              your last breath?

Our Llasa Apso plays sentry for the inner palace,
       as his ancestors did, outside
              our bedroom door.

By all accounts of animal shamans here
       and in the next world,
              he should have been dead by now.

He takes his cue from the High Llama and views
       the world from his perch
              at the top of the stairs.

We can hear his beard grow at night.

still moving

At the garage sale I watch silk roses, pale with pink
edges, wave goodbye like my former life heading
down the driveway with how many years left?

Stripped of its yellow slipcover,
the couch blends in with the wallpaper,
and a side chair looks forlorn.

My oaken desk, refinished by me,
hand-rubbed with its dents and scratches
so noble you can put your feet on it,

staggers under files, candles, books
and I can't yet imagine it cleared off
when my son comes for it.

How many changes can one being bear
from family of origin to breakup of a home
loss of matriarchs, patriarchs, dissolution

of the familiar once more, children suddenly
grown, and now a fifth wheel headed south.
A woman wanted to buy my couch,

after her truck is repaired, after she
rear-ended a man on I-35, after she
goes to Arkansas for her sister's

birthday, after her biopsy (may be cancer).
The fragments of her life are understood.
The woman never came back.

Ninety inches wide, modified colonial,
the couch saves the curve of my body
when it held me between its arms

one endless night. It sits anonymous
in the sudden space of the living room,
until some relatives pick it up tenderly,

carry it to the end of the driveway to wait
for the truck from the school for the blind.

IV

As we ponder life expectancies,
the cold labyrinth of numbers,
I look across at you and see that
we are vulnerable and realize
again that we are not immortal.

We talk at the kitchen table
with my former colleague
who sells long term care,
euphemism for the short term,
the likely last two years of life.
She and I were teachers, members
of a "terrorist organization,"
so named by the Secretary of Education.

Papers filed, we set out, our used
fifth wheel hobbit house behind us.
We spend our first overnight in Amarillo
beside an interstate. Ah, the camping life.
We uncork wine, toast ourselves,
the traveling life, and any life
hereafter for us, together.

As we lay our heads upon new pillows,
the drone of trucks come from the past,
into the eternal present, and on
to what we call the future,
and we are lulled by this to sleep.

You dream that you testify at a celebrity's trial.
I dream of teachers who stand up to fascists

who run the school where I work.
One body is recovered from water
in the beginning. We take off
our brass chains and badges
and put them in a pile. Other teachers
on their knees, arms forward, are tortured
each time they resist. Fingers chopped off
systematically woke me to a Texas wind
and dust that wants to cover us all too fast.

You have made tea and unwrapped cakes
on blue place mats. It is morning.

minorities

At the neighborhood store, a monopoly
business crackles with a target market:
rice, frijoles, tortillas, lard, Mexican bread.
Tight jeans, tank tops stretched to the limit,
brown babies with Mestizo eyes steal your
gaze, seven-year-olds bounce soccer balls
beside Grandma, Aunt, Mom, Dad, children
of history's cradle swell, move, fly, careen
into the future like a rocket on the Fourth,
taking the family with them, ready or not.
Two Anglos look for green tea, low fat stuff.

happy palms

As far north as Canada, people jumped into a Midwestern
funnel and headed south. When they arrived here
they said, *ten minutes from the border, 45 from
the island, far enough.* Women with strong arms
volunteer for kitchen duty and dance night
or both. Former farmers, pipe-fitters and
their wives, people from cold winters
long nights, play shuffleboard and win
despite stiff backs and hands. War
vets, engineers, women who can
fix anything gaze at you with
a strong eye, ready to lead
to any card you think
you are big
enough
to hold.

two transplants

Three orange trees surround
our camper at one end,
drip with fruit that once

saved sailors. Last night's wind
shook oranges to the ground
the Great Grackles with their

Spanish tails will pick at later.
Clay chimes on a table
attract a jackdaw, beads

above the chimes mistaken
for food or accepted
as a source of entertainment.

He leaves when I tap the window
but not before he tilts
his head to show me

his pale eye and ambition.
He brings back a friend
to pick at the fallen fruit,

and he eyes the clay chimes
on the table once more.
Why did we come here?

A question that ignores fresh
fruit, resents the beauty of pushy
birds. We pick the precious fruit

and breakfast on it each morning.
We narrow possessions
like the birds and orange trees.
.

now odon

This time of day the birds
and road noise do battle.
Chimes join the soundtrack
and life takes on the likes

of an old DeMille epic
with a garden from central
casting: Garbo and Gable
stroll near the trees, stop

for a cigarette. Bogey flirts
with Bacall at the Hibiscus.
Errel Flynn foils the bad guys
with a cast of thousands.

Two hummingbirds shoot past
like bullets, one chasing the other.
Sugar water for all yet they take
turns, torment each other.

A mockingbird competes
with quarrelsome sparrows
and the wounded sound
of doves floats against heaven.

My partner hammers near my nook
as if to design new sets,
and a small lizard stares at me
with its ancient, yellow eye.

16 | SHIRLEY RICKETT

car watcher in a power wheelchair on a busy street

for Larry Stone

Someone he probably doesn't know
honks and waves. He waves back.

What is he thinking?
About the NASCAR races he lived,

dredged up by the traffic drone,
the picture-taking, the trophy and kiss

in front of the checkered flag,
especially the kiss?

The stroke from some mad design
seldom far from his mind, he says,

a brush with an opening gate,
its yawn ready to swallow,

that wave that pulled his mouth aside
to make his speech mildly tortured,

but we could always understand
his favorite greetings—

"Hi, hi, hi …
Hi, whacha doin'?"

borders

Cacti once planted by someone
becomes a memory of order,
of border aesthetics, but
Nature is blind to history.

The growth along the fence,
a barrier to the street,
jungles a small forest.
Each plant competes for the sun.

The orange tree gives and gives
as long as we water it.
Volunteer trees of unknown
origin line up along the fence.

A battle rages here
in the quiet, in the sun,
in a garden intended to be
someone's gentle back yard.

Deprived of sun, two cacti
turned the color of an old penny,
have gone limp, stand lost,
their chlorophyll, succulence gone.

A small yucca traded green
for death, part faded jade.
A cactus nearest the sun, yet
still in shade begets small green

paddles as if to say, *I'm still here*.
Tumbling over the fence, red
Bougainvillea plunders the scene,
blankets more cacti and reaches

across the grass. It is coming this way.

the birds at happy palms

The arc of one note's ascension
ends with a question mark
above our heads, then another
until the stripe of each grackle call
trumpets interrogation
against the blue vault.

Minutes away from the Gulf,
we have answers in place here,
like the man who said he knew
four thousand songs and would take
requests as he stood on stage
dressed in Johnny Cash black.

Even the one-note birds
cannot reach the ears
of angels like the silence
that rises from people
who stand erect as the body
allows, hands on hips
or walkers, while they watch
the ambulance leave
and turn up its violent song.

post christmas in the valley

In Kansas City we fed-exed one gift
back to ourselves, to the place

of return, we, like the orb
in a pinball machine

hitting wickets until we exit.
The plane cabin writhed—weary

passengers, fussy babies, luggage.
How do they ever launch it?

Home again—just north of the border—
the clock with numbers

fallen in one corner
laughs at time. We laughed

when we opened it,
read the word *whatever*

above the dainty black hands
that point to nowhere

as we searched for a familiar corner
to fall into like the numbers six and four.

I don't know my home

Once I thought it a lake cove
sleepy with frogs in summer,

frozen in winter, a scene
with geese paddling the one

open space, taking turns
to keep it open for each other.

My birthplace is dust now,
parents gone, my birth state

alien. The state where I lived
most of my life continues to tug

my sleeve from miles away,
unravels threads I thought firm.

Missing are the ruins, where
are the ruins, the excuse for

absences? Inside a gray church
yard where comfort never was,

or can it be a neighborhood where
streets tower with huge elm trees,

a song that pushes me into the street,
or an empty house dusty with dreams?

the people at table twelve

At a distance I saw my friend smile
        as she came toward me
                with a face radiant
as when she was a young girl.

I know this because her soul
        came across her face
                holding a light
that roamed into her eyes.

A man we were with moved through
        a crowded restaurant
                in search
of a table for four.

He turned, and as we moved
        toward his signal
                his soul seeped into his face
to be present that mundane moment,

chosen that second by the cosmos
        to transform the years, the rather
                plain face with a big nose,
to one of beauty and smoothness.

The soul seeks travelers.
        It doesn't mind distortions
                caused by PTA meetings,
divorce and other deep loss,

or how many politicians
        it takes to change a light bulb.
                The soul loves to change us,
change the way we look,

even if only for a whiff of time.

good friday

Evening sneaks in like a child from bed.
Porch lights light. Birds quiet.

Here, the day ends like water slows
to wet the rocks near the river.

Time, that old fool, laughs at me again.
Today a hummingbird took a bath

near the sprinkler. Its feet are so small
it can't see them. Yesterday

the newest Pope kissed and washed
the feet of women. The purple cloths

will come down in the churches Sunday.
Most everything confessed once again

suspends sin in a bell tower.
The statues will speak and tears

will wet their feet. Stars in their beds
will open windows soon. At dawn

Jesus will shine like the sun, be the sun,
and we shall kiss the wounds

in each other's morning hands
in the earth near our hummingbird feet.

a cool easter

Yesterday people shivered
and walked the stations
of the cross in Basilica park.
Small groups moved from

scene to scene that changed
like leaves from season
to season. What comfort
to pray at a saint's feet

or look upon a cross
with a wounded man
you know will rise up
in eternal spring of green.

Wal Mart sells chocolate eggs,
yellow marshmallow chicks.
We buy a bowl of soup at the Deli
on Holy Saturday, admire the babies
and toddlers with dark hair
and bright eyes. Ours is a field
of uncertainty, the silence

between the stations. Former
tinters of eggs, masters of stealth
and change, we offer thanks
and drink in the warmth here.

how to move in the world

The shape of a life
is the form
that carries it:

fins or dimples,
eyes—the way in,
collection of bones:

the carriage of it all
dictates boundaries.
Form moves in

purposeful walk,
seductive dance,
running away from, to.

The mind's soft tree
floats
holds reason
and temptation.

the real auntie em lives at pleasant grove

She lived in Tennessee
her whole life and now
closer to her late years
we visit her in her one-room
schoolhouse—bought
for one dollar—she widows in.

Clark Gable, Joan Crawford
and the like make her wallpaper.
Starched doilies arc on tables
in the parlor. They talk
to each other whenever she hums
or sings in her tiny soprano.

Four feet tall, she is ever alert
for sample shoes (size 4)
to take her to church across
the dirt road from the house.
Her chickens roost in trees
and she is happy to see me

and my children leave.
Veronica Lake peeps
at our luggage. The doilies
strut in their sugar starch,
and whisper, *city slickers*,
and the hens will now lay again.

self talk

Stick your hoary head out the door.
Do you still hear flaming music

or are you better off inside?
How the days come down so slowly

and so fast ripping out your life.
Those black and white pages

from old movie calendars
are coming for you, coming for you.

And what have you done? Count it.
Make it good for it's all you have:

This isn't dress rehearsal.
The oldest fears live on.

You can avoid thinking
with the ten o'clock news.

Thinking is the problem,
dreaming even worse. Hamlet knew.

What sum of years have you done this?
Each mind sifts the same sand.

It is good to have sand to sift,
a corner to sit in, a place to go,

a small lamp inviting joy.

peeling a papaya

Dig the knife
into leathery skin
into flesh the color
of flaming sunset, red,
peach, orange,
coalesced into one color.
Slice and pile your sunset
on a plate
until your knife
meets the center,
the temple of the gray pearls,
and you shall know wealth.

.

official buildings

Take a number. Have a seat.
You will meet with an official
Presently. Have your papers
Ready. Driver's license, SS,
You are a number after all
And we are here to serve.
Ah, you've been here before.
Hours are posted on the door.
Do not go past this point
Until your number is called.
The only thing that changes
Are the pictures on the wall.

rancho lomitas

At the ranch of the little hill,
a climate change happens
in less than a mile. Dry air
to moist: breeze, a new direction
for a blessed few square feet.

A plant points its leaves down
in the morning as if to tell
the soil *my leaves are flat
and green*. Leaf fingers
turn silver afternoons, point up
to say something to the sky.
This is a mystery lost to the wanderer
who passes by twice, believes
in two plants instead of one.

2

Pucker brush some people say
to dismiss brambles, mesquite,
cactus, berries, foliage green
and grey, life and the living.
The wanderer could eat
blue-green algae, cactus fruit,
certain roots and stay alive out here.
Prickly pear cactus maintains
glucose levels, lowers LDL
if a person lost in the wilderness
cares. Dead mesquite, buffalo grass,
and maybe a little mud makes a shelter.

Leave that indigo snake alone—
it eats rattlers.

3
Like a miner waking up
screech owl pokes its head
into the world
from a box
the size for bread.
The news spreads fast.
Five people stand below.
Owl's head and ears suggest
a child's tangled hair.
We want to see the rest of you,
hope you'll get out of bed.
We don't know what you think
of us. You watch us look at you.

4
In the dirt road
small rocks
mark an oval
like a message.
*Look for a coin-sized
depression* says the guide.
Like children
on a field trip
we look in the powdered dirt.
He lifts
the trap door
with the blade tip

of a pocket knife,
draws a map in the dust
of the underground tunnel.
The spider stays home
like an old lady.
She is tarantula-size, he says.
Another trap door
tampered with
and legs come out
close the door

Coyotillo grows berries (kiyo tiyo)
that hold seeds that paralyze
the consumer. Benito knew
coyotes ate the berries
and could still walk and run,
unlike the farmer's goats
who ate the berries
and couldn't walk.
Benito took coyote scat
and rinsed it, found
the seeds intact. Coyotes
ate the leaves, swallowed
the berries whole
and stayed strong.
The wanderer must be
smart like coyote.

.

somewhere in south texas

Memory floats out of reach
in a pool circled by palm trees,
bodies surrounded by water,
blue arch overhead for cover.

Family far away like a dream—
still we heard the crack in Greenland.
Not a tree say the inhabitants,
but ice that is Greenland's own dance,

the thing Greenland mostly is.
Yet here we float with memory's kiss,
unable to fly there, offer a band-aid
for the newest terror the dark father made.

Nothing seems real but the blue of the pool,
the contrast of tiles, water that soothes.

breaking news

A truck loaded with sunflower seeds,
an eighteen-wheeler, slid off the ramp.
five lanes closed. Police & this
reporter tried to stand on the exit ramp,
the hill below & above. The seeds
of a single flower, favorite treat
of birds, genesis of sunflowers,
thousands, whole fields upon fields,
confounding us as we slip and slide
in our confusion with nature,
germination, transportation, news,
& the fertile possibility that some things
we do grow into our biggest mistake—
Back to you, Kate...

taking pictures of people taking pictures of fields of sunflowers

Tuscany, 2009

The backs of people with cameras
sprout arms at angles, careful arcs.

Legs genuflect in half-squats.
The box they hold, the spell it casts,

their trust in it, can replace
grief and loss, doubt and fear

in one piece of an hour.
Here we all are, digitized

mesmerized by fields
of yellow glory. We learn

joy in being, when we see how
the flower faces follow

the sun from the first stab
of morning to melted evening

light, to some new form
of god now become our secret.

not your kentucky bluegrass in south texas

a ghazal

Down here, I'm told, grow two kinds of grass—
St. Augustine, my yard's fate, or Bermuda grass.

This saintly stuff would strangle my plumbago.
Sand-binder for games on turf makes Valley grass,

a root-system made in heaven or Darwin's book.
Root-fingers beyond control weave this grass.

No pear trees here but a few citrus orchards left.
Beings speak in the scant orchard grass.

I long for the blue-green fringe of old home.
Light and fine were the feathers of that grass.

Angels spoke in my yard, in my past.
Beings below ground birth *this* grass.

Entities whisper to the tangled under-part.
Underground whispers drive up blades of grass.

Long and short spikes reach for light.
The reach for light becomes the grass.

I want to know those whispers underground.
I want my name on each knife-blade of grass.

we came from underground

Pueblo, Hopi

The ancients believe people emerged
from under the earth through a sipapu.
Life down there was crowded and difficult.
Some left with followers, even the whites,

up through the Grand Canyon,
trouble-makers and witches supposedly
left behind. Some children sank in water,
became kachinas, ones who wear masks.

You must make your own mask,
or have someone make it for you, sort of a trip
to the tailor for something special. You wear
the mask for social events, certain dances.

You must not sell your mask for a part of you
is in it. This must be confusing in Washington.

.

interval

When the spring shower ends
the sun creeps out, not full
but half-hearted, and the light
lies in a glow on the grass,
and sparrows take on the color
of eagles. Mockingbirds shake
the mist from their feathers like
Quetzalcoatl preparing to sing.
Puddles mimic lakes, a mirrored
look of bright lead in a dream.
A yellow hose coils by a carport.
The fig tree bears new green fans
low on the trunk where the frost
didn't reach. The sun comes

    out full, mystery leaves.

.

eyes wide open

*The name of a national exhibit of boots from dead soldiers who served in
Iraq that soon became confined to state exhibits due to increasing numbers.*

We arrive at the park early and wait for the van with boots.
They come in plastic bins, boys' boots, men's boots
with tags, names alphabetical, then town and state.
Some bear daisies or sunflowers stuck inside

that bump against the leather.
Letters and poems dangle from laces.
I read one dead man's thoughts, his life in Iraq,
his daily agony, his hopes and fears, stare at

the photo of him in fatigues kissing his baby.
Where sorrow and grief live and resist,
more must be endured. We set out the boots,
measure with yardsticks one yard apart both ways,

but the boots are different sizes like unruly boys.
Bend, measure, place, adjust. Order—we must have it
in death if not in life. Our director repeats the exhibit
in towns all over the state: *The rows must be precise.*

She struggles with angles, with volunteers.
Just eyeball it she tells me after we shift a row
for the fourth time, after we all join her angst
to get it right, get this one honor right.

The soldiers stand at attention, ancient and worn
with eyes wide open, blinded by history and war.
The rows of boots tremble in a triangle on the green.
Next to them a jazz band unloads at the outdoor stage.

evening news

At the end of the news
comes the pictures
and bios too short
to mention a life
or even to say
he was here, she was here.

Proud or funny faces,
often a uniform,
sometimes not,
then grieving hands
can't find that photo.
If you squint
you might see them
playing with a dog,

holding a baby,
perhaps at a graduation
a camera in hand,
or at a reunion
the glass of wine
a few inches from the lips.

the exile

for refugees everywhere

Come now to the quiet glade
then the street where men hold
up body parts for the world to see.
Take a drink of water.

It is good.
Watch longing grow
into a charred night
a piece of bread

a star-smeared sky
without city lights.
Your place is the long road.
Love is in this line for you.

There is no beginning.
You were always there
in desire, in the idea of home
that place you reach

for every day through
the bars of your cell
in your steps in the dust
your stops, your rest.

waiting

Jean François Millet
Nelson Museum and Art Gallery

The mother steps toward the open road,
her body a question mark,
her outward step fierce,
her lean to the road a challenge

to time and chance.
In her mind an image of her son
must materialize on the rise
in the road ahead. He grows taller

as he comes toward her until
his whole self is in view.
She must go to meet him.
Old Tobit, framed in the doorway

of the stone house, looks like
an ancient tree that decided to walk,
one foot still in the house,
the other hovers above the ground

over the raised threshold.
He is blind. He carries a wooden cane.
No one else sees their vigil,
only spectators, voyeurs,

with arms folded across the chest
or hands held behind a back.

the camps

A prison that's a melting pot:
Whole families live among these camps,
the people everyone forgot,

or people no one knows about,
employment for the poorest towns,
a prison that's a melting pot.

Some say it's true that guards mock
two-year-olds in uniform,
the people everyone forgot.

Child, lay your head upon this cot,
never mind your will to play
in prisons that are melting pots.

"'Catch and release' didn't work,"
the mindless drone of bureaucrats
on people everyone forgot.

Tent or wall, barbed wire aloft:
"Line up" several times a day,
in prison that's a melting pot,
the people everyone forgot.

Immigrant detention camps in Texas:
Pearsall, Los Fresnos, Raymondville, and Hutto

.

moad kansas july

On a Monday evening, people
sit around two tables slid together
in a pizza parlor, nine people,
the number frozen in the a/c air
like the words widow and odd number.

The town's handsomest boy and girl
take a seat in a corner booth.
They are the idea of beautiful.
They bring the lost nectar to town.

The waitress chats with a customer,
her voice, a foghorn, her nicotine fingers
stained like her vocal chords must be.
She shifts her weight in worn sneakers.

As we leave, a hot wind straightens the flag,
blasts us, makes us bend forward
like the few soldier trees left standing
on this prairie as if they were left here
to mourn the loss of the young.

peace

Doves coax a voice contralto,
feathers in the throat, the same
one heard at the customer service
desk, or where war is constructed.
The sound pattern, paisley,
locks in the trees before dawn,
the time of attack or judgment.

Some doves mourn the loss of night,
beg forgiveness for sins for which
they cannot account. They converse
with heaven moonstruck soon to be
dumbstruck for they bear the burden
assigned by faith-healers and generals,
pieces of laurel beneath their feet.

things

It is in the life of things
we live without force.
Vaguely the flame lifts
from the candle
and our own warmth
makes its home there,

retraces the waver
our steps took
to come this far.

We know candle
and flame, child
and parent silent
in the same sentence.

We remove our shoes
at day's end and leave
on the kitchen table
our last scrap of paper.

.

dressed in new clothes
truth goes incognito

Truth blinds opponents with itself.
When a folksy politician meets
with a family at the kitchen table

chasing it, claiming it, Truth
goes out the door in search
of the perfect cup of coffee.

We lunch on it and know it not.
It sleeps in the one real carrot
in your soup, unannounced.

Someone in the next car
gives you the finger.
You pretend it didn't happen.

A walk in the park refreshes.
Maybe there is some still left.
Half of the news comes on.

You try to fall asleep. Morning:
you find Truth evaporated
with the night. Make breakfast.

.

shadow

In honor of Clarissa Pinkola Estés

Not the long one in lamplight
the visible one but the interior one

who causes all the trouble
how not to be kind

how to self destruct
things you try to avoid

most every day, except
the wild woman, who let's

a woman live for herself.
Beware. Go there. Listen.

Her voice is charcoal gray
lit with black diamonds

she pushes at us.
Without her amoral calling

some of us might not be here.
It took so long to know her.

Like Vermeer
we must mix our own colors.

.

red

A palm tree waves to me
like a woman's long hair in a breeze.

Bougainvillea, never satisfied, has climbed
the small tree next to it, then the cactus,

red in places reserved for the powder
of clouds, the mockingbird nest.

Who can blame it? Across the way
a pine tree humbly accepts the assault

and red claims branches that lift
with prayers from hands of stigmata.

This famous color invades dreams
when they're shadows of gray and black.

Film noir keeps the lid on tight,
hides Carmen's skirt in the habanera,

When red comes, and it will, open the gate,
start the music, smell the grape before you drink.

late afternoon

Car tires lap at the road
behind our home, a sound
of near then far with
the regularity of clocks.

Children must be collected.
Dinner must be reviewed.

The sun sends its rays
in stripes on the thick
grass. Birds grab
the last nervous
insects of the day.

Plants stir in a breeze
that was wind
this morning, the one
that sweeps us into
the numbness of habit,

the comfort of ritual.
Late afternoon nurtures
the winding down of the day
into evening, the tender
shoals that bring the night.

.

by guadalupe river

Kerrville, Texas

When day eases into last light,
several deer with young graze.

Six necks stretch and freeze.
We stop on the trail yards away.

They resume feeding and we don't move.
This trust suspends our breath.

We want to touch them, stroke them,
but the distance is great; the light fails.

Soundless they fade into a thicket.
We trudge up the hill toward lamplight.

sugar cane

Down in the valley, the valley so low …

Someone said the other day
that the big cities call this place
the armpit of the state. When
sugar cane burns, its curls of ash
annoy those on shuffleboard courts,
swipe at wet sheets on the line,
will smear a black char on clothes
if touched. Few notice the cane burn
unless its pylons of smoke rise up
and people who winter here see it
from cars, or point in a vague
direction.
                              The origin
of the ash is lost in the ash itself
as it takes on the shape of houses,
jackdaws, and small dark men
who bend to their work.

.

first dove of summer

Fat, brown, and gray, it sits on the garden trellis,
bloats its chest with the call of love, lust, or something

old and sad. Wings tremble; tail feathers shake,
and this is only the beginning of the old story

when the dove got its call from a sad troubadour
and lost its shoes on the way into town.

Another call from across the way and it's saved.
The two of them tune up for summer's grip

and dream, our slow unrest, our navel-staring.
They voice the sound of loss, the last thick thrusts,

crumbs in the forest left by the brother and sister,
or is it Aida's rival, Amnaris? Soon the trees

will be thick with mezzo-soprano sounds of power.

an island where a world begins

South Padre Birding and Nature Center, August 2013

The sun sits on our heads, a heavy hat in August.
It's afternoon siesta for some marsh birds,
the Roseate Spoonbills, the color of a newborn's cry,
the others mere blobs of white, Monet brushstrokes
from where we stand. An alligator lazes in cloudy water.

Minnows flash silver, then black—swim in schools,
ready prey for something else that must live. Green jays,
dune meadows, pelican and peregrine, huisache blooms
at the southern tip of the world's longest barrier island.

Impossible to know this world, its secret
of teeming life everywhere, layers
present from the first day. We sit
dumb in the bird blind with a sea breeze.
Three kinds of gulls swoop above us.

A brown duck with five babies knows we cannot reach
them from our boardwalk path. They huddle in the grass,
a breath away from water. Can they smell our sweat?
Do they sense the alligator mere yards away?

Laguna Madre to the west, Gulf of Mexico to the east:
The skirts of the mother sweep a way to life,
the pattern of her gown, waves of seagrass,
the arch and scent of turtle.

after hurricane ike

Padre Island National Seashore, 2008

A four-mile stretch of trash,
debris once purchased,
(except for a small palm tree
and an octopus preserved in a jar),
a section of roof, a hot tub,
a happy snowman in a lifejacket,
a grinning plastic pumpkin, wash up.

It's everything, people's lives,
says a marine scientist.
No laughing matter, says the snowman
and the jack 'o lantern.
Kemps Ridley turtles
will soon struggle to dig their nests
among things people wanted,
things people thought they needed,
delivered with each high tide.

.

allotment

Reading poems
one eye on the timer,
or the timer watches me.

Food and poems—
which is reality?
Routinely, someone cooks,

someone works, the shape
of food and work
restates itself in image,

the shape of food
on the plate—
transitory—the meal

gone, the finished
work, fresh when new,
may hold up or not.

But the memory,
oh, the memory
of work, a meal,

making something,
goes on with each tick
of the timer.

.

in the dermatologists office

Bandaged like soldiers patients wait—
patches on chins, arms, heads—
for the pathologist's eye at the slide,
the shrapnel of age and sun their lot today.

A teen boy sleeps in his chair—
his mother attentive to the form
she fills out. The vital statistics
of the life she gave him flows

from her pen legalized with insurance
or the lack thereof. An office phone
sounds like a one-note bouncing ball
among a steady mix of Spanish

and English. A toddler shrieks, bored
with the ennui of waiting rooms.
All the seats are filled. The people who
just came in must stand. They find

something irresistibly funny and try
not to laugh as they convulse, turn away.
Hammer of sturdy heels on tile—door
to the inner sanctum opens on a spring

and St. Peter's envoy pronounces
a name. Guilty, we are all guilty
but we are in the right place. The toddler
dances forth while we all watch.

after you left

for Nancy

Each morning it begins all over
you said, like caring for a child.
The mediocrity of feeding, bathing,
can drab a life, or earn the famous
hanger of routine, the comfort
of knowing what to expect each day.

In your purple world, this labyrinth
with its sieved light, stray ease
tools the mind, the heart to move on.

I think of you and your patience,
your cheeriness, your masterful
solutions without a trace of bitterness,

and I wish we had seized more days
to roam the town, stop for lunch
with wine, look for ourselves in windows.

maría luisa

A voice crackles in Spanish
on the phone—no it's English
with an accent big enough
to challenge any gringo.

Am I coming to teach tomorrow?
Do I need anything? Will I ...
María Luisa slows her words
as I answer in kind, slowly ...

María Luisa who hugs and kisses
me every time I see her. María
who calls me *teacher* who loves
to learn, who now teaches others.

poetry reading

Room mellowed with low light
as if for clandestine operations
poems enlarged   mounted on easels
to make them louder   students
filter in like inductees   to find
a seat   visit   quell nerves

imagine auras like birthdays

Welcome ... the mayor regrets
he couldn't be here tonight ...

We are not really Mestizos anymore ...

the lights dim   poems
rise like flowering plants.

This is a hip-hop poem titled,
'Discrimination' ...

We are Abercrombie and frijole ...

faint jazz music   murmur   cocktail
party ambience   punch and cookies

with wealth measured by laughter ...

family and family and family

We have become war-mongering fools
downloading IPOD tools …

please write comments on cards
about your favorite poems tonight.

… to survive one nation under racism
with amber waves of greed …

and we thank you all for coming

creative writing class

Four women sit in chairs
next to daycare noise
notebooks on laps.
They weep at what they write.

great blue heron

Assuming nothing—lifting
wings that resemble winter
light cast only on certain
days—it flew to the
other side of the cove
shopping on the way.
I watched on shore
and felt like a stranger.

.

quinta mazatlan

Quinta: country house
Mazatlán: Land of the Deer

Next to a golf course, across
the street from the airport,
a few blocks from the mall,
lies a green forest in the city,
a few acres of old world,
Tamaulipan Thornforest:

cactus, mesquite, thorny underbrush,
      river-bound wetlands, el Rio Bravo,
          and what used to be South Texas,
ninety-five per cent gone, where
      chachalaca, kiskadee, green parrot,
          ocelot, reptiles, piece a famous garden.

They soar, these birds, above the land,
      the city, and markers show the spot
          one spot, and down they go.

Who knows how the ground creatures
      smell the green, the water, the thorns, the bush?
          They go. They find it.

etude

My darling, in my mind,
in what my thought became,

you remained in the house,
yet stayed beyond those windows.

The sun and its idea leans
through green leaves as I realize

you've already left on your
errand, the echo of your voice

a chime, and I am caught
in a morning of our lives.

in living every day

In the life of things our loved ones leave
a vision in the remnants of living:
She hands her coat to him to keep
evidence of return, of being.

His yard shoes and jacket lie casually
near the back door as if he will arrive
any moment to fill them naturally.
He has gone to the store for limes.

She will enter the kitchen, retrieve
her watch, pick up the damp dish towel.
His book remains by his chair,
testament to the life of nouns,

images become sacred,
silence become record.

what holds

This wine glass, this fork
I take inside with a bag

of papers, books. What do we
practice here among the trees

as the sun creeps down
and evening arrives, a slow

sweet thing? You are the center
that holds for me and if I leave

before you, please know, this night
in early Fall is all I could ask.

my husband washing dishes

He makes the same sounds that I do,
the knocking of bowls

against a stainless steel sink,
the clatter of flatware like horses running

on pavement, yet, his hands, somehow,
go deeper than the sink and water goes everywhere.

His hands, so gentle, so thick,
leave the country,

celebrate every pair of hands
that ever dived into suds,

grateful for the extravagance
of water, the joy of soap.

on the back porch

I want to go where the sky bends no more,
where I can invent the next horizon.

Two teen boys pass by, their laughter
mezzo, contralto, with flashes of baritone.

A car with the heartbeat of a giant-killer
thunders along the back road intent on desire.

The gulf breezes sing with the chimes
and I am somewhere in between

listening for voices gone to me,
lost like shabby notebooks hinged

on breath and purpose. Whatever hope
I'd resurrect left like Texas dust

in the wind. My suit of skin
holds a child, a woman, a crone.

It gets crowded in there. Take apart
this body and believe stardust will win.

Give me one more evening where the kiskadee
looks down on me and shows its yellow suit.

the bell inside

The future lies at our backs
say the Chinese. Only the past
lies before us. No wonder
my dumb self cannot see
or speak these days.

Study the garden I tell myself,
watch the sparrows feed
below the Tibetan bell.
Hope that seed and chime
and night when it comes
will push your dreams awry
to some intelligible scheme
some juice of the mind
to imagine another new life
not blind to the stars
the bulbous moon
the folding Hibiscus at sunset
the awful unfolding in morning.

Fear is only fear.
That view of the wide time
before us, where memory seeps
through here, there,
with my father's crooked smile
my mother's stance at the stove,
cuts tiny windows, not much more.

When all around me sleeps
I hear the bell chime in a breeze.
The one inside answers.

awake at three am

with thanks to William Stafford

Even in the deep fur of dark
and sleep the world cannot be
held off from the mind
from dream to waking place.

Where is that switch
for the small light
under the kitchen cabinet?
Yes, it's all here. Your life,

or what you call your life
from time to time.
Beloved books, the beloved
asleep in the bed beside

your indentation.
Then comes the silence,
the low hum in the house
and you know how

you cannot save anything
or anyone. You may never
truly know another person.
You breathe in and out

and find comfort
in this breath, in reading
the words of another,
in the rolling out of words

on the page, in this open
corner of the world.

possum in a cage

It seems to debate free will and fate
with its noble snout, eyes that test
this new present tense, its labyrinth
tail at rest on the cage floor.

Come close. It commences
a sway ever so slight side to side
born of the tyranny of fences.
It prepares to defend, engage.

The cage lays bare the wild to naked—
eyes move to depths uncalled for;
time on strike questions why in its blanket
we are still here, it is still here.

a wall of windows

for Charles

He resets windows
      that barely rested in slim
settings of board and nail,

      This wall of windows will greet
eastern light, frame the yard
      with its live oak and palm.

His carpentry and breath all this day
      blend to mix our lives
welded now, light as rectangles.
      Our yard of heaven burns bright

as his industry. Is it he or I
      who imagines morning
through that glass in this new place?

yard

My yard is the one
my mother always wanted.

She would pick at tired
Irises, the one Rose of Sharon

bush in our pitiful
treeless acre,

a field with a house.
Even the grass was sad.

Her history of land—
cabbages, corn, and dust—

never shed from her feet.
I make her bed every night

in the sky where her window
opens on this yard,

sub-tropic bleating plants,
a catalog of birds,

and she bears that look
of wonder every morning.

where we live now

I said home, said, back home.
After the visit, going home,
back down home, said, I'll leave
this at home, when I meant hotel
or I'll stay in the guest room
at my son's home before
I leave for home, that place
in the mind, on the road,
destination always changing.

I'm thinking home and me,
home and us the same.
My children means place
and home of the past, and now
their homes; they live here,
we live there, under cover
of self, wanderers of place
not knowing home, except
when together for a while,

       or an old friend
I haven't seen for years
feels like coming home.

road trip

Hello again, road, with your dotted line
to nowhere. Sky, hello, a new horizon
where ever you end.

Hello granaries
for towers of old gold gone to mice teeth,
the last of refineries, a few dying towns,
hello to those who stayed.

Hello farmers with grapevine hands,
your empty dawns, your saved seeds
unmolested. Hello, cattle and churches

county fairs, crochet and milk, chickens
and canning and quilts, my grandma
and your aunt and uncle,

Hello Texas,
Oklahoma, Kansas, the Flint Hills,
Missouri with your meandering river,
rolling hills, ponds, lakes, trees, trees,

trees! And the sons and daughters
of today, tomorrow, wary of crows
what will you leave us this time …

last leg

driving Texas to the Valley

Long, the state from top to bottom.
The map congests itself with veins
and the splotch of the bigger cities.

In downtown Dallas folks of color
wait at every bus stop. Sports cars
pass—long blonde hair, shades, or

sleek gray hair, a quiet BMW.
Buildings mirrored to catch the souls
of those who come and go, reach up.

The freeway becomes highway.
A road straight south points ahead
with hardly a grass blade there

on the map. A tiny town down here.
The maniacal traffic is gone. Grass
and trees wave to us. The landscape

changes, the people turn brown,
descendants of those who crossed
the ice bridge, who settled South

and West, and to where we go, earth
without maps in the minds of people,
a niche for frail new roots.

breath of words

Reading a poem out loud
in the quiet of a room
in late afternoon—

the porch chimes sing
in the smothered hush of the fan
and the roll of word rhythms

release the rush of breath
carve it out as waves
cram it through the walls

and the fall and the rise
of the poem forms
its own water and air,

becomes the breath of millions
listening to the waves as work
stops, traffic slows, minds change,

while the poem goes on
in its own weather
to well-kept lawns

and the tiled-roof houses,
the crumbling trailers,
dirt yards and broken things,

to the mirrored beach where lovers
embrace in the foamy water
and the seagulls laze

in the boiling sun. Reading a poem
in the quiet of a room
in late afternoon swells the breasts

of trees and the kisses of leaves.
The words and the breath
take on the whole world.

how the world grows old

If we knew the best of love
would the chasms between us

fill with beautiful horses
that rush back the night—

Would the armies of the world
stop and go home—

Perhaps the wisdom and joy
that flowers in each new rise of children

would cause them to help prepare
the table for the family meal,

the slowing of the great clock,
the last caress and glistening eye.

the best part of a new year

may be its very blankness,
what we call the future,
always on the brink, less
abstract than before, nurturer

of emptiness, tuned shapeless shape,
measured in the year we hope
to take that trip, refine our days,
accept that pain lives in the boat

we call the body, and that
leeward drift allows respite, your
stiffened hands still magic craft
and nothingness holds more.

The heart comes forth in a wave,
jeweled water takes its leave.

author biography

SHIRLEY RICKETT moved to Missouri from east Tennessee as an infant in her mother's arms. The history of her family and her birth-state remained with her as she grew up, went to school, married and lived one lifetime. She and husband Charles retired to South Texas to embrace another ground, another climate, another culture. *Transplant* is her first full-length book of poems.

other titles from
VAO PUBLISHING

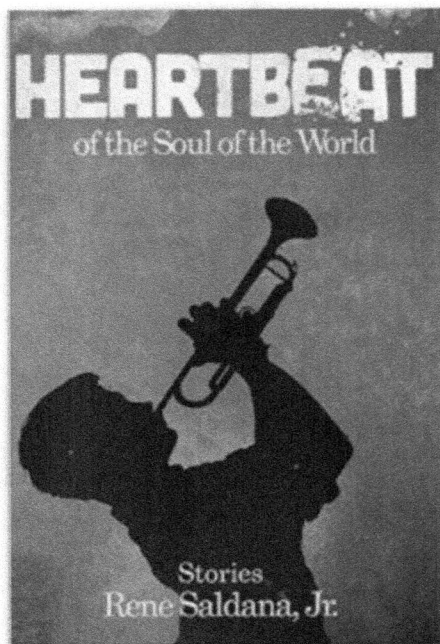

Heartbeat of the Soul of the World
Stories by René Saldaña, Jr.
ISBN: 9780692412039
Juventud Press

A young man finds his voice in jazz, leaving a mark on his community that will never be erased. Another discovers his words in books and carves them into angry poems. Bullied kids at the end of their rope are given friendship and protection, while other teens cannot clear the hurdles life sets in their way. And at every step the promise of love glows bright even in the gloom of teenage life. In this new collection, René Saldaña, Jr., echoes the rhythmic pulse of life along the border. These brave, nuanced, accessible stories—ten previously published and five new—will resonate with young readers everywhere, especially Latinos. Come. Lean in close. Listen to the heartbeat of the soul of the world.

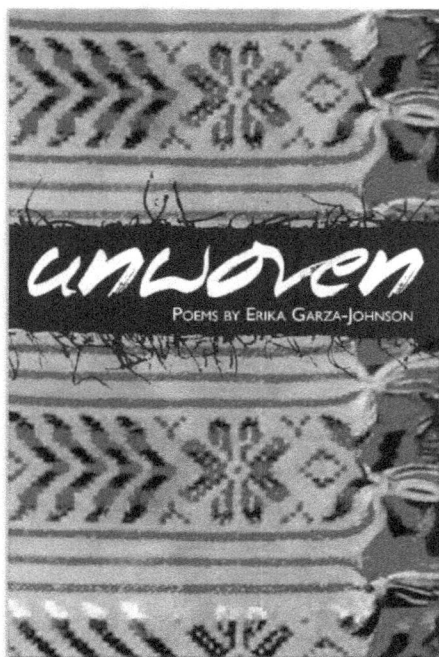

Unwoven
Poems by Erika Garza-Johnson
ISBN: 9780692323908
FlowerSong Books

The first poetry book from one of the most distinctive voices in South
Texas, *Unwoven* is an unflinchingly honest exploration of Chicana
womanhood along the border, a scattering of quetzal feathers and jade that
celebrate the achingly lovely paradox of life on the edges and in the middle.
Playful, artful, and wholly memorable, these poems prove Erika Garza-
Johnson deserving of her enduring moniker: *La Poeta Power*.

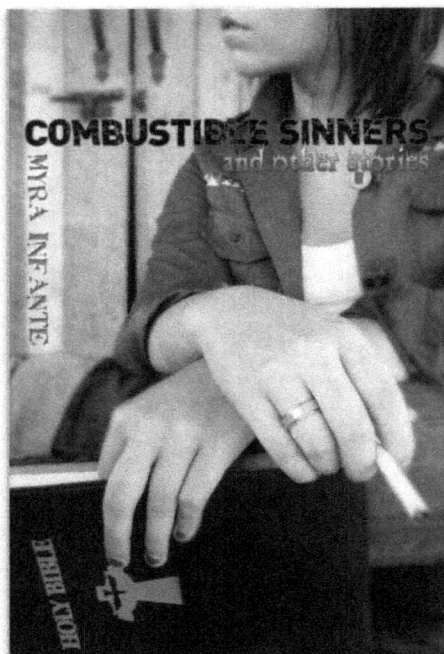

Combustible Sinners and Other Stories
by Myra Infante
ISBN: 9780615556703

Lissi Linares is a pastor's daughter whose love for others contrasts with her fear of eternal damnation. Little Jasmine "Jazzy Moon" Luna is determined to save Jesus from being crucified. Naida Cervantes hides a brutal secret behind shapeless, florid dresses. Hermana Gracie tries to set her son up with a good Christian girlfriend, only to make a surprising discovery. Zeke wants a new guitar and Ben wants a cool girlfriend, but what they find as migrant workers in Arkansas changes their desires. These individuals and others try to negotiate the often rocky intersection of faith and culture in seven independent but intertwining tales that explore life in an evangelical Christian, Mexican-American community. Frank, funny and heart-breakingly real, this volume explores themes of identity, culture, religion and sexuality in the context of a little-known subset of Hispanic culture.

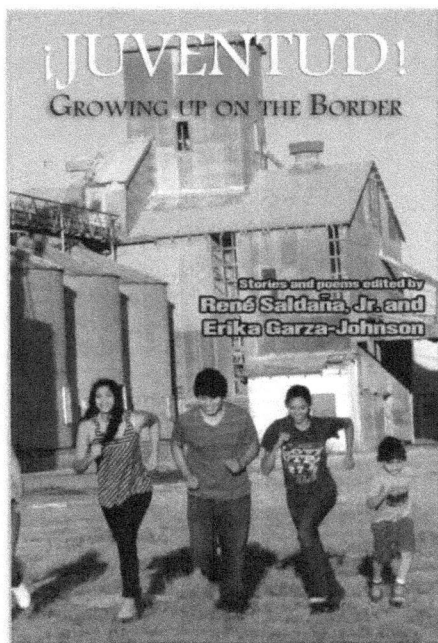

¡Juventud! Growing up on the Border
Edited by René Saldaña, Jr., and Erika Garza-Johnson
ISBN: 9780615778259

Borders are magical places, and growing up on a border, crossing and
recrossing that space where this becomes that, creates a very special sort of
person, one in whom multiple cultures, languages, identities and truths
mingle in powerful ways. In these eight stories and sixteen poems, a wide
range of authors explore issues that confront young people along the US-
Mexico border, helping their unique voices to be heard and never ignored.

Featuring the work of David Rice, Xavier Garza, Jan Seale, Guadalupe
García McCall, Diane Gonzales Bertrand, and many others.

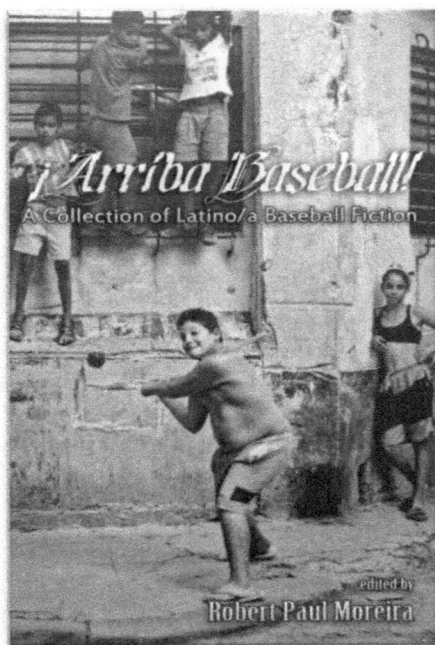

¡Arriba Baseball! A Collection of Latino/a Baseball Fiction
Edited by Robert Paul Moreira
ISBN: 9780615781839

From Dodger Stadium to the Astrodome, from the Río Grande Valley to
Chicago, from Veracruz to Puerto Rico, from high-school teams to stickball
in the streets, from the lessons of fathers to the excited joy of daughters,
from massive cheering in the stands at Wrigley Field to the dynamics of
family and community echoing on the diamond, these fifteen stories use the
sport of baseball to explore geographical, cultural and dream-like spaces
that transcend traditional notions of the game and transform it into a
universal yet wholly individual experience.

Featuring the work of Dagoberto Gilb, Norma Elia Cantú, Nelson Denis,
Christine Granados, René Saldaña, Jr., and many more.

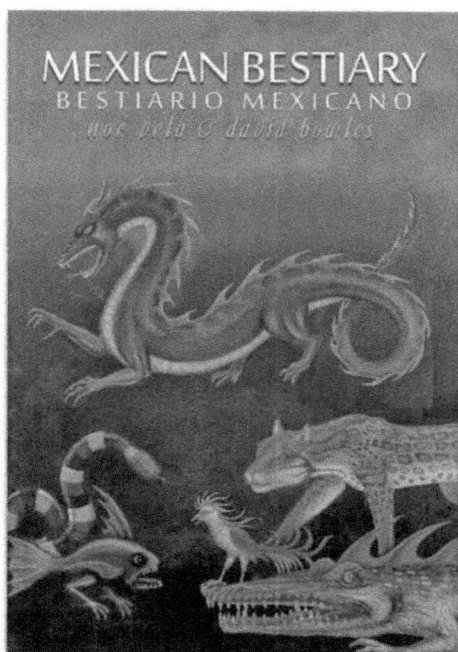

Mexican Bestiary | Bestiario Mexicano
by David Bowles and Noé Vela
ISBN: 9780615571195

Who protects our precious fields of corn? What leaps from the darkness
when you least suspect it? Which spirit waits for little kids by rivers and
lakes? From the ahuizotl to the xocoyoles—and all the imps, ghosts and
witches in between—this illustrated bilingual encyclopedia tells you just
what you need to know about the things that go bump in the night in
Mexico and the US Southwest.

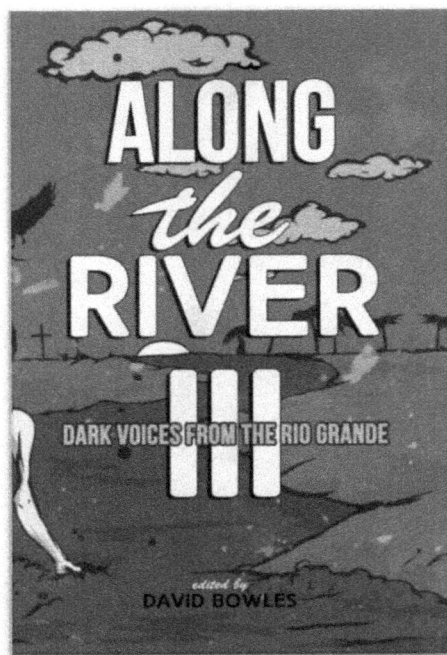

Along the River III: Dark Voices from the Río Grande
Edited by David Bowles
ISBN: 978-0615956183

The third anthology in the _Along the River_ series.

When the sun sets on the Río Grande Valley, all manner of dark voices begin to croak, snarl and wail. Come explore the black shadows amidst the mesquite and palm trees down at the water's edge…just have a care not to fall (or be pulled) into the current.

Featuring the short story "Niño" by Álvaro Rodríguez.

FLOWERSONG BOOKS nurtures essential verse from the border-lands. A division of VAO Publishing, the imprint is named for the Nahuatl phrase *in xōchitl in cuīcatl*—literally "the flower, the song," a kenning for "poetry."

VAO Publishing is a division of the 501(c)(3) non-profit Valley Artist Outreach. Our mission is to promote both the voices of writers in the Río Grande Valley and the literacy of Hispanics in general. To achieve these goals, we are implementing a multi-tiered strategy:

- editing an annual anthology of local talent (*Along the River* is the name of this series)
- publishing a small number of titles by Valley authors (or by authors whose work would appeal to readers in the Valley) each year
- procuring top-notch authors to edit anthologies of established and upcoming writers whose work has special relevance to the Río Grande Valley
- providing creative writing workshops to aspiring local writers
- conducting writing contests for elementary and secondary children

www.ingramcontent.com/pod-product-compliance
Lightning Source LLC
Chambersburg PA
CBHW031537040426
42445CB00010B/588